12 Days

Of

Christmas

Devotions

12 Daily Devotions

By

Megan Hodges

Day 1

Your Journey through the Seasons

To everything there is a season, and a time to every purpose under the heaven. Ecclesiastes 3:1

As the earth journeys around the sun, it experiences seasons. Some are hot, some cold, some that bring new life, some that bring rest, change, renewal.

The same thing happens in our lives. As we are on our journey, our lives must revolve around the SON.

We experience seasons as well. Seasons of testing, trial, renewal, new life, new relationships, changes, new priorities and goals.

Every single journey has changes. Every journey has highs and lows, ups and downs.

If you take a physical journey from one location to another, you will have to walk up hill or downhill. Your path will wind in different directions. Sometimes your path will go through the sun or through the shadow.

The point is, every journey will have good and bad. If you decided you no longer want to walk on your journey and you stop, you won't make it to the next season, the next hilltop, the next spot of sunshine.

The only way to get to the next season is to keep going.

You must continue moving forward. Nothing will last forever, we all know this. That means that the bad spot, scary path, steep hill you must descend, will be over soon.

Soon, you will be headed back up that hill to the sunlight.

Just keep moving your life around the SON. He will bring you through all of your seasons and He will do it with loving perfection

Lord, as we enter this Christmas season, this season of giving and festivities and fun, let us remember the true reason we are able to experience it all. That reason is You, Lord. Help us to take You with us as we move into a new journey and very soon a new year. Help us to let our lives revolve around You. As we are busy with gifts and parties and snowball fights, let your wonderful gift of salvation never be far from our minds. Help us to take time to celebrate You. Amen.

Day 2

Season of Giving

...It is more blessed to give than to receive. Acts 20:35

It is the holiday season. The season of giving. But....

Is it just me or has it become the season of buying? The season of sales and shopping and camping outside of shopping malls when you are supposed to be getting your beauty sleep?

Yes, I know you are shopping for gifts for other people, so technically you are giving. But really, I think Jesus wanted us to give something much more than can be wrapped with a bow.

He also wants us to give of ourselves. He wants us to give time, hope, love, encouragement and most of all Him.

He wants us to share Him and His love. Christmas is supposed to be all about Him after all.
So while it is wonderful to give gifts on Christmas, let's not forget what we should be giving all the time.

Don't get so caught up in having the fanciest decorations and the best gifts under the tree, that you forget we are supposed to give as examples of Christ.

He didn't walk around with big bags of gifts and cookies. He walked from place to place giving life, love, hope, comfort, joy and Himself. The greatest gift of all will always be Jesus Christ.
Praise Him for His marvelous gift!!!

Let's make extra special effort this year to make it a season of truly giving, not a season of buying and comparing and competing.

We have been given unimaginable gifts! Grace, Love, Mercy, Salvation! So let's pay it forward!

Give a lonely person your time. Pay for the person in the drive through behind you just because. Give up your spot on the bus. Do someone else's chores just because you care. Give grace to the negative person who always bothers you. Turn off the TV for a night and just enjoy someone's company. Tell someone they are beautiful. Pray with someone.

Take a moment every single day to make sure you have done something because it is the giving season and you want to follow Christ's example.

Lord, let us take time for others today. Help us to appreciate the gifts around us. Give us the grace to look beyond ourselves and give to others. Help us to look beyond our own problems and give to others because You have given to us. Amen.

Day 3

For unto you is born this day in the city of David, a Savior which is Christ the Lord. Luke 2:11

It's Christmas time! I love this time of year.

Getting to spend time with family and friends. Buying gifts for loved ones. The excitement when I watch them unwrap the perfect gift.

There is only one thing I don't like about this time of year, however.

The reason for the wonderful celebrations held all over the world seems to be forgotten. People run around and buy gifts and decorations and trade recipes and go to school programs and don't seem to stop for a small moment and think about why we celebrate.

In case anybody reading this doesn't know... I believe in Jesus. I believe He is the Son of God, born of a virgin to become the Savior of us all.

I believe that Christmas time is a time to celebrate Him and the wonderful gift He is to us.

Yes, we buy others gifts as a testament to the gift He is to us, and how much we love them.

But, I think this time of year we should strive to focus on the real reason we can celebrate this holiday at all.

The birth of Jesus Christ.

So, while you are shopping for gifts and going to parties and programs, please don't forget to take time just for Jesus.

Tell Him you love Him. Tell Him thank you. You can even tell Him happy birthday if you wish!

Christmas is a time of love and laughter for many. But, let it also be a time of worship this year.

After all, we are celebrating the birth of the One who gave us the greatest gift of all.

Lord, let us celebrate You today. Help to stop running and shopping and decorating for a moment and just be thankful for who You are and what You have done for us. Help is to realize the time we spend with You is more important than any sale, program or decoration. Amen.

Day 4

Decorating an Empty House

Let your light so shine before men, that they may see your good works, and glorify your Father which is in heaven. Mathew 5:16

At Christmas time it is always fun to drive around and look at all the houses with fancy Christmas decorations.

Big, bold, bright attractions that say "Merry Christmas" and "Seasons Greetings."

When you see these decorations on a house it is easy to tell that someone lives there and is proud of it.

No one is going to decorate an empty house. What would the point be?

Well, guess what?

When we trust in Jesus, He lives in our hearts and we become His home.

Just like you can tell someone lives in a house by the effort they put in to decorating, we should make the effort to let people know Jesus lives in us.

When people notice us they should be able to say "Jesus lives there."

Is your heart home for Jesus?

Are you proud to let people know He lives in you?

Or, are you just wasting time trying to decorate an empty house?

Lord, help us to let our light shine for you today. Help us not to focus on the outward attractions, but the love we have for You in the inside. Help our love for You be what people notice about us this Christmas season. Amen.

Day 5

From Sorrow to the Savior

And there was one Anna, a prophetess…and she was a widow…which departed not from the temple, but served God with fastings and prayers night and day. And she coming in that instant gave thanks likewise unto the Lord… Luke 2: 36-38

Anna was a prophetess, a great woman of God. Before she had become this, however, she went through a great period of sorrow.

Anna was married, in all probability quite young, and just seven years after she married, her husband died. She was left a widow at a very young age and with very few options.

Anna chose to work in the temple. She could have gone back to her family or let her husband's family take care of her, but she chose to stay in the temple. That was quite a choice she made as such a young woman; to devote herself to living for the Lord, alone, for the rest of her life. The Bible even says that the rest of her life was a long one.

…she was of great age, and had lived with a husband seven years from her virginity; and she was a widow of about fourscore and four years… Luke 2: 36-37

She had been married for 7 years and then widowed 84 years. If she married as young as 14 years (which was not uncommon) Anna could have been 105 when this story takes place.

Because of her faithfulness and dedication to God, God decided to give her a special gift. She would get to meet the Messiah. She would get to meet the baby, born of a virgin, whose coming was foretold by the prophets of old. She got to witness a prophecy fulfilled with her own two eyes.

She met the Savior.

The Savior had just been born in Bethlehem days before and His parents were bringing Him to the temple to be circumcised and to offer sacrifices to the Lord. As soon as Anna found out they were in the temple, she instantly ran to meet them. God had let her know the Messiah had arrived.

Because she gave the rest of her life to God she was blessed and shown favor. In fact the name Anna actually means "favored by God." How amazing that God put the name "Anna" into the mouths of her parents before anyone ever knew these amazing things would happen!

Looking back at the beginning of her life, Anna was introduced to sorrow. Years later, that sorrow became the reason she was able to meet the Savior. If her husband had not died, she would not have stayed in the temple and, therefore, never met Jesus.

Sometimes the greatest of sorrows can be turned into the greatest of joys. This lonely widow was able to meet the new born King of the Jews, the Savior of the world, just days after His miraculous birth. All of this happened because she experience sorrow in the begging.

My friend, if you are going through a sorrowful time, take heart. Do not give up on God. Just because something difficult is going on in your life does not mean that He is done with You! God made have even greater, more miraculous things in store for you; but you must remain faithful to receive them.

Anna had to wait many years, but I am sure she rejoiced over every day she had to endure because she was one of the very few who were able to see the Savior.

God worked miracles for Anna, He can work them for you too.

Day 6

No Refunds No Exchanges

*For the wages of sin is death; but the **gift of God** is eternal life through Jesus Christ our Lord. Romans 6:23*

I get a little nervous sometimes when I go shopping for someone else. Whether it is for Christmas or their birthday, I always second guess what I am buying. I hope they like, love, want to keep it, enjoy it, etc...

I usually try to get a gift receipt just in case I bought the wrong gift.

I cringe a little when I go shopping and I see something I really want to buy for someone and there is a sign that says; "no refunds, no exchanges."

But what if I am wrong and they don't like it? What if it is the wrong size? Or what if they end up with it at a white elephant gift exchange and the gift is totally not "their thing." (that has happened to me quite a bit)

Or, have you ever found out that someone re-gifted something you bought for them? That doesn't feel great does it?

There is a gift, however, that I know will be a perfect gift every time. Jesus.

Giving the gift of Jesus to someone is something that will never be returned. It is the ultimate gift; so you can never exchange it for something better.

My grandpa was preaching one night when I was young and explained very clearly what a gift Jesus was and how I needed to receive Him.

What good is a gift if someone tries to give it to you and you never accept it? I knew that I needed to accept Jesus. A few nights later, I knelt beside my bed with my daddy and I asked Jesus to be my Savior and accepted the best gift I could ever and will ever receive.

What is also amazing about this gift is I hope that everyone I give it to re-gifts it. That's right!! Pass it on to whoever you please.

It is a gift that will never be too small, too big, too expensive. You can never be the wrong shape, color, age or size to accept it.

Once you accept Jesus you will never want to give Him back. He will always be just right for you.

So go ahead; shop 'till you drop, decorate with ribbons and bows, exchange gifts all you want.

Just don't forget to give and be grateful for the best gift of all.

Jesus.

The reason for the season. The hope for tomorrow. The lover of your soul.

Lord, thank you for the wonderful gift You are. Thank You for loving us and sacrificing Yourself so we can receive the gift of salvation. Help to love You so much that we cannot help but pass this gift on to others. Amen.

Day 7

What would you say?

Blessed be the Lord God of Israel; for he hath visited and redeemed his people. Luke 1:68

☐☐☐☐☐☐☐☐☐☐☐☐☐☐☐☐☐☐☐☐☐☐☐☐☐☐☐☐☐☐☐☐☐☐

Zacharias was a man of God. He was a good and faithful man, but like all of us he had the potential to doubt God. This was evidenced when the angel Gabriel showed up to tell him his wife would have a baby and he argued with the angel.

He thought for sure his wife was too old to have a baby. His punishment for doubting and arguing was that he would be unable to speak until the child was born.

Nine months. Unable to speak.

When I play the quiet game with my Sunday School kids they can barely make it two whole minutes before all the words they want to tell me come bursting out of their little mouths.
Now, Zacharias gets to play the quiet game for nine months. He even got to speak with an angel face to face and couldn't even tell anyone about it!

Good grief. I bet that was rough for him to not be able to speak for that long.

Could you imagine all the things he wanted to say? All the thoughts he wanted to share but opted not to because finding a tablet and writing them was just a pain? I'm sure he was very frustrated.

But then the time came. The baby was born. As soon as Zacharias confirmed the baby was to be named John, the name God chose, he could speak. The Bible says "his tongue was loosed" and he could now communicate openly and verbally. Nine months of waiting and now was the opportunity to share everything on his mind. Instead, he chose to praise God.

His first words after his angelic encounter, were words of praise to God. The God who gave him a miracle baby. The God who blessed his wife. The God who took away his ability to speak.   Instead of being mad or confused, he was praising.

What would your words be? If you had lost the ability to speak for a while, what thoughts would you be aching to express?

Would they be thoughts of love? Frustration? Anger?.... or praise?

God knew Zacharias needed some time to reflect on those things. Zacharias used it wisely. He proved it by praising God at the first opportunity.

What would your first words be?

Lord, during this season of giving, help us to remember to watch our words. Help us to trust You and obey You so we can live the best life. Help us not to hinder ourselves by not exercising or expressing our faith. Amen.

Day 8

One Savior Fits All

*But we see Jesus, who was made a little lower than the angels for the suffering of death, crowned with glory and honour; that he by the grace of God should taste death for **every** man. Hebrews 2:9*

*Therefore as by the offence of one judgment came upon all men to condemnation; even so by the righteousness of one the free gift came upon **all** men unto justification of life. Romans 5:18*

One size fits all. When I see items advertised that claim to be one size fits all I usually laugh out loud or roll my eyes. It is almost impossible for a product to come in a size that can actually accommodate everyone.

Imagine sitting on a train and looking at the people around you. Then you pull a sweater out of your bag that says one size fits all. Do you really think it is going to fit everyone on that train? Probably not.

Sometimes people make outrageous claims that if you buy that item, it will be a gift that can benefit everyone, when most of us already know, it really won't.

But, there is one man I know that has given a gift that will work for absolutely everyone. The Savior, Jesus Christ. His gift is one Savior fits all. And let me tell you, it fits.

His gift is a heart gift, a soul gift. His gift is salvation. It doesn't matter how tall you are, how short you are, how old, young, stubborn or smart you are. Your size, shape and color have no bearing on the gift He desperately wants to give you.

He died on the cross to give you the gift of eternal life wrapped with the ribbons of His precious blood. His devil shaming, heart healing, soul saving, life giving blood. Praise Him!

What an amazing gift! The one gift that is truly a fit for all.

Lord, thank You for providing such a wonderful gift and making it available to all. You could have chosen only a few. You could have chosen not to give a gift at all to such an undeserving people. But You did. You did! Praise You, Father! Help us to live grateful. Amen.

Day 9

Why the Shepherds?

And she brought forth her firstborn son, and wrapped him in swaddling clothes, and laid him in a manger; because there was no room for them in the inn. And there were in the same country shepherds abiding in the field, keeping watch over their flock by night.

And, lo, the angel of the Lord came upon them, and the glory of the Lord shone round about them: and they were sore afraid. And the angel said unto them, Fear not: for, behold, I bring you good tidings of great joy, which shall be to all people.

For unto you is born this day in the city of David a Saviour, which is Christ the Lord. Luke 2:7-11

As a child, when I heard about or read about the story of Jesus' birth, I would wonder why God sent angels to tell the shepherds.

Of all of the people God could have chosen to receive an angelic message, why them? Why not announce in it some grand, amazing way to everyone!

Instead, God chose a few lowly shepherds in a field outside of Bethlehem.

I used to think it was an odd choice, until now. I was reading the story of the birth of Christ just the other day and the thought occurred to me that shepherds were the perfect choice!

Shepherds lead their sheep, protect their sheep, feed their sheep and keep their sheep close. Sheep also have very specific needs. A sheep's nose is created in such a way that the water must be still in order for the sheep to drink.

"..he leadeth me beside the still waters. " Psalm 23:2

The shepherd is also known to chasten the sheep when it goes astray in order for it to learn to stay close to its master.

The shepherd keeps watch at night. Even the longest, darkest night will not stop a shepherd from watching his flock. It is his duty to protect them at all times. Even during the dangerous times, a shepherd does not leave or stop watching over his flock.

A shepherd also knows all of the sheep individually and exactly how many sheep are with him. The shepherd will also risk his life and make sacrificial choices in order to save a lost sheep or lamb.

Jesus is our Great Shepherd. Jesus leads us, protects us, loves us, knows us and wants to keep us close. He watches over us in the night. He never sleeps or stops watching over us. He also gave His life in order to save us, His sheep.

Now I do not question God's choice at all! Who better to hear the wonderful news from the angels then the shepherds. They were blessed to see and hear from angels, rejoice with them and go to Bethlehem and see Him for themselves.

There he lay, in a manger, the Great Shepherd. The Lamb of God, who came to lead us and save us from our sins!!

Lord, help us to remember how amazing the story of Your birth really is. Don't let us forget the awe and wonder of Your life here on earth and the sacrifice You made. Thank you for being our Great Shepherd. Thank You for loving us, protecting us and watching over us. Amen.

Day 10

The Chosen One

And the angel said unto her, Fear not, Mary: for thou hast found favor with God. And, behold, thou shalt conceive in thy womb, and bring forth a son, and salt call his name JESUS.
Luke 1:30-31

I don't have any children, but I do have a baby nephew. He is my favorite. I love him to pieces. Just being able to hug him makes my day.

I am not even his mother and I could not imagine just handing him over to someone and saying "Here, take him and raise him" but that is exactly what God did.

He knew that His Son would have to go to earth to die for the people, but He had to choose just the right person to raise Him.

Now, I don't know about you, but I'm pretty sure God would not have picked me to do that when I was as young as Mary was.

He looked through the earth and found her to be the only one qualified to handle birthing and raising His one and only precious Son.

Not only did He give Jesus to Mary, but He gave Jesus up for 33 years! That would be so tough for any parent. I know my sister has a hard time when I babysit my nephew for a few hours.

She is always texting me and checking in on him and when she gets back she picks him up as soon as she can. She loves him. He is her heartbeat. She is his mother.

God knew that He needed someone who would live Jesus like that. He needed a pure, innocent woman, who already loved Him and would obey Him no matter what.

Mary was surprised by the news the angel gave her (of course) but she also trusted God and vowed to serve Him and obey Him through it all, which she did.

God has a special task and needed a special person to carry it out. Mary was that person. What a gift!

This doesn't just stop with Mary, however. Each of us was made for a specific purpose as well. Maybe God has a special task and is looking for someone just like you to carry it out.

Will you run away? Will you deny him? Or will you, like Mary, accept it with grace, obedience and courage?

Stay strong in your faith and obedience to God. You never know when He will be looking for someone just like you.

Lord, let us be obedient to You. Give us the grace and wisdom to be chosen when You have a special task for us. Help us not to live our lives in a way that will disqualify us from being used by You. Thank You for Your willingness to give us chance after chance to serve You. Amen.

Day 11

Christmas in a Box

"Thanks be to God for His unspeakable gift." 2 Corinthians 9:15

Christmas time doesn't last forever. At some point Christmas time will be over and January will come bringing the New Year with it. That will be the time everyone starts packing things up.

Trees, ornaments, nativity scenes, ribbons and bows all get packed away in boxes for another year. Forgotten for another year.

Unfortunately, will all of the lights and decorations, the spirit of Christmas often gets packed away as well. The spirit of love, giving, gratitude, thoughtfulness and worship.

Christmas is a celebration of Jesus and the way He came to earth to save us. While Christmas day is only one day a year, the spirit of Christmas and celebrating Jesus can stay with us each and every day.

Everyone morning that we wake up is a new opportunity for us to worship Jesus and spread His love to others. Just because we wake up in a month that is not December, doesn't mean we have a right to forget about the wonderful way God cares for us and the gifts He gives all year long.

So as we prepare for another year around the corner, let's prepare our hearts to celebrate Jesus each and every day...not just in December.

Lord, thank You for Your amazing gift and the season of celebration we get to have each year. Help us to keep that gratitude in our hearts throughout the year as well. Help us not to pack away our awe of You will the boxes in the attic. Help us to use each day as an opportunity to appreciate You. Amen.

Day 12

The Perfect Gift

...the gift of God is eternal life... Romans 6:23

If you are anything like me, you love giving Christmas gifts.

I love picking out that perfect present for someone, wrapping it up and waiting anxiously to see their face when they open it. It is just so much fun for me to know that I am giving them something they want or need that they normally wouldn't get for themselves.

But, no matter how much I plan, prepare and purchase, none of my gifts could ever compare to the gift God gave us.

Jesus.

He sent Jesus down to earth to be born of a virgin and then to be the ultimate gift for us.
Jesus died for our sins and made a way for us to get to heaven. Because He loves us so much, He gave us the gift of eternal life in heaven. All we have to do is choose to accept it.

Give the perfect gift to your loved ones this year. Tell them of God's gift to each of us and show them the way to Jesus. He is, after all, the reason we celebrate this season.

Merry Christmas!!

Lord, help us to remember what an amazing gift You have given. Help us also to realize the responsibility we have to share this gift with others. We share recipes and coupons and news of sales, but we don't share You like we should. Forgive us and give us a new sense of responsibility and gratitude. Thank you for Your indescribable gift. Amen.

Would you like to receive this gift?

Step 1- Admit that you are a sinner

For all have sinned and come short of the glory of God. - Romans 3:2

For the wages of sin is death; but the gift of God is eternal life through Jesus Christ our Lord. Romans 6:23

Step 2 – Believe that Jesus is the Son of God who died for Your sins and rose from the dead.

For God so loved the world that he gave his only begotten Son, that whosoever believeth in him should not perish, but have everlasting life. John 3:16

But God commendeth his love toward us in that while we were yet sinners, Christ died for us. Romans 5:8

Step 3 – Confess your sins and Call on Jesus

That if thou shalt confess with thy mouth the Lord Jesus, and shalt believe in thine heart that God hath raised him from the dead, thou shalt be saved. Romans 10:9

Seems pretty straight forward, right? All you have to do is pray a simple prayer following these steps to ask Jesus into your heart. If you would like to accept Jesus as your personal Savior, pray this prayer:

Dear Jesus, I thank you for your marvelous gift. I believe that you died on the cross for my sins and that you rose again. I am so sorry for my sin. I pray that you would please forgive my sin and come into my heart and be my Savior.

That's it! That is all you have to do. If you pray that prayer believing in Jesus He will save you. The Bible says:

"For whosever shall call upon the name of the Lord shall be saved." - Romans 10:13

"That if thou shalt confess with thy mouth the Lord Jesus, and shalt believe in thine heart that God hath raised Him from the dead, thou shalt be saved." - Romans 10:9

That's all you have to do. God loves us. He means it. So, please, take some time to read this over. If you are not sure you are going to go to heaven, please think about this carefully. It is God's desire that each and every one us is able to go to heaven. If you have read this and want to be saved simply say the prayer above.

12 days of Christmas Devotions by Megan Hodges

Strivingtoserve.com

Made in the USA
Las Vegas, NV
11 December 2024